My Gingin Roots

Some Early Pioneers of Gingin, Western Australia

Kay McCashney

My Gingin Roots
Copyright © 2021 by Kay McCashney

All rights reserved. No part of this publication may be reproduced, distributed, or transmitted in any form or by any means, including photocopying, recording, or other electronic or mechanical methods, without the prior written permission of the author, except in the case of brief quotations embodied in critical reviews and certain other non-commercial uses permitted by copyright law.

Tellwell Talent
www.tellwell.ca

ISBN
978-0-2288-6626-8 (Paperback)

Table of Contents

ACKNOWLEDGEMENTS AND FORWARD 1

BACKGROUND TO THE ESTABLISHMENT
OF THE SWAN RIVER SETTLEMENT IN
WESTERN AUSTRALIA 3

RICHARD EDWARDS 1777-1850 and ELIZABETH
TUMBINS/TOMLINS 1784-1866 12

MATTHEW EDWARDS 1825-1916 and ANNE
(ANNIE) KING abt 1835-1879 33

JOHN YORK 1812-1896 and ANN ADAMS 1811-1897 42

RICHARD (CONSTANT) KING 1799-1891 and
ELIZABETH ANNE GARDINER 1806-1883
(Was known as Ann) 52

JOHN THOMAS 1829-1920 and MARIA
BUCKINGHAM 1836-1919 55

THOMAS BUCKINGHAM 1808-1879 and MARY
CHANTER 1814-1875 63

SUMMARY 69

ACKNOWLEDGEMENTS AND FORWARD

I wish to acknowledge the awesome family history research carried out by my mother Maud Thomas. Mum did this research at a time before the internet existed. There was very little general interest in the area of family history at that time and so much of her early work was done by letter to churches in England and I can only marvel at how she persevered and kept all the information together as she built her stories. She presented her work in a book entitled "From Horse Age to Space Age" which essentially is a book written to her grandchildren about their ancestors. This book is available thru the State Library of Western Australia.

Much has changed since Mum's time and new information has come to light which has filled in some gaps and changed some of her findings, but the major bulk of her work remains as she established it way back last century.

After Mum died, I inherited her work and became fascinated by the area and have pursued it ever since. I have also expanded into the DNA area and during this process, I have had the privilege of connecting with some long-lost cousins – hello Sandie, Lara, Owen and Lyn – and in 2017, along with cousin John and family, we spent an enjoyable weekend together, exploring the old historic homesites in the Gingin area. There have also been family trips to the area at various times with my two siblings, Noelene and Allan.

I also wish to acknowledge the help of my sister Noelene who proof read the chapters and offered valuable suggestions.

The impetus for this book occurred when, at some point, I realized that all of my ancestors on my paternal side, came out from England to Western Australia very early in the colony's history and all of them ended up in the Gingin area. I thought this was pretty amazing and decided to write this little book about them. I hope you enjoy it.

Any mistakes in this book are entirely mine. I have no doubt that in the future, new information will come to light and may show further inaccuracies in my work. If you find inaccuracies, please feel free to contact me as I am always updating my information,

Kay McCashney 2021
kl.mccashney@gmail.com

BACKGROUND TO THE ESTABLISHMENT OF THE SWAN RIVER SETTLEMENT IN WESTERN AUSTRALIA

Let's set the scene in the new country to which our ancestors set sail so long ago and try to understand what their experience might have been.

Calder (1977) describes how the settlement in Western Australia was characterised by hasty decisions largely based on a desire to beat the French rather than a considered approach to the establishment of a new colony. The early settlers were ill informed and unprepared for the harshness of the land to which they were heading and Stirling's glowing report of a land with rich soil and ample water was misleading to say the least.[1]

However, before we look at the Swan River Settlement, we need to understand that this was not the first British settlement in Western Australia. In 1826 Governor Darling despatched Major Edmund Lockyer of New South Wales to King George Sound (Albany). His instructions were to set up a military outpost with some soldiers and a small convict working party. Lockyer arrived

---

[1] "Early Swan River Colony" Mary E Calder. Rigby Ltd., Australia 1977

on the "Amity" on November 9th 1826 and established what was called "Friederickstown".[2] Again, this appears to have been in attempt to beat the French. Both the military and the convicts were withdrawn after a few years leaving a few hapless settlers to struggle on alone there.

Long before this however, the first known European to set foot on Australian soil was Dirck Hartog who, on Oct 5th 1616 landed at Dirck Hartog Island, Shark Bay, Western Australia[3]. Hartog left a pewter plate nailed to a post which recorded his visit. His ship was the Eendracht of the Dutch East Indies Company. It is interesting to me that if you ask most Australians who was the first person to 'discover' Australia, most people would say Captain Cook who navigated the Eastern Seaboard of Australia but in fact the Western seaboard of Australia had been known and chartered by the Dutch much earlier. Later in 1697 William de Vlamingh on the ship Geelvink, found Hartog's plate, removed it and set another one in its place. Vlamingh sent the original plate back to Holland. A replica of this original plate together with a further inscription stating the facts of the Hartog and Vlamingh plates can be found at the Cape Inscription Lighthouse which stands close to the site of the original plates.

The idea of a new Swan River Settlement in the 19th century however, was based on a much grander vision of Captain James Stirling. Captain Stirling had visited the Western coast of Australia, or New Holland, as it was then known, in the "Success"

---

[2] "A Story of a Hundred Years: Western Australia 1829-1929" edited by Sir Hal Colebatch C.MG. Fred W.M. Simpson, Government Printer Perth W.A. 1929

[3] Swan River Booklets No. 6 "The Story of Dirck Hartog: the first white man to land in Australia Oct 25th 1616 Cygnet. Published Paterson Brokensha Pty Ltd., 65 Murray St., Perth 1929

in 1827. He and his party explored some 80 kilometres up the Swan River and produced a glowing report of a "rich and romantic land" page 16, and by 1829 he had persuaded the authorities in England to establish a small settlement there. This was done largely because of concern that the French might do the same. The British Government however had no intentions of spending a lot of money on this venture.[1]

On Dec 28th 1828 Stirling was advised that he was to be in charge of this new settlement. He requested that 'possession' be taken of this land prior to the arrival of the settlers. The "Challenger" under Captain Fremantle reached Cockburn Sound April 27, 1829 to do just this. A second ship the "Parmelia" was to carry the officials of this new settlement, along with their families and provisions. The "Sulphur" was to carry a detachment of the 63rd Regiment under the command of Captain F.C Irwin. The Parmelia anchored in Cockburn Sound on June 1st, 1829 with the Sulphur following on June 8th.[2]

An influential syndicate of monied men, which included Thomas Peel, had proposed to send 10,000 migrants from England, Ireland and Scotland to the Swan River. Each male migrant was to be allocated 200 acres to grow tobacco, sugar, flax and drugs. Horses were to be bred for the East Indies and cattle were to be raised for the British army, navy and the mercantile marine. The Home Office rejected this scheme as being too ambitious and proposed instead a modified version involving a million acres of land. Half of this was to be allocated to the first 400 migrants to arrive at the colony and the remaining half to be allocated to subsequent migrants.

The original syndicate did not accept these terms and it was dissolved. Thomas Peel however decided to continue the venture himself and on Jan 28, 1829 informed the British Government that he was prepared to go ahead with the modified scheme. The British Government agreed but tightened the conditions. The first grant of 250,000 acres would be contingent on him landing 400 settlers at the colony before Nov 1, 1829. A further one million acres would be allocated as subsequent settlers under the scheme arrived.

The proposal to establish the Swan River Colony was widely advertised in the papers in England with emphasis on two outstanding advantages. One condition was that no convicts or prisoners were ever to be sent there and the second was the granting of free land. The granting of land was contingent upon the land being improved within three years. This must have seemed very attractive to some aspiring citizens of England.

Among the earliest landholders in the W.A. colony between 1829-1932 were many members of the middle and upper middle class of England. There were doctors, lawyers and sons of professional or landed gentry. Also included were retired officers of the Army and Navy.[4] Leonard Easton in his book "Stirling City" ((page 7) quotes W.B. Kimberly "Substantially Western Australia had for its pioneers, more highly educated men of good society than perhaps any other British dependency".[5]

Peel set off with three ships, the Gilmour, Hooghly and the Rockingham. Unfortunately, they were six weeks late, with the Gilmour arriving Dec 15th 1829 and so missed the deadline set by the British Govt. By the time of their arrival, Stirling had already allocated Peel's land to others and he declared that the grant was

---

[4] "On the Swan" Bourke M.J. University of W.A. Press 1987
[5] "Stirling City" by Leonard A Easton. Stirling City Council University of W.A. Press 1971

now void. The passengers on the Gilmour were disembarked on the coast near Woodman's Point and the site was named Clarence. The second ship Hooghly arrived Feb 1830 and many of these passengers lost their possessions in a fire soon after they arrived. Finally, in May the Rockingham arrived.

It was within this scheme and on the Hooghly that our first ancestors Richard Edwards and Elizabeth Tomlins arrived.

The Hooghly set sail for the Swan River colony on Oct 25, 1829 with 180 emigrants aboard. They left from St Katherine Docks, towed out by the "Dart". The captain was Peter Reeves and the Second Officer was George Bayly. We are extremely lucky that the second officer on this voyage was Mr George Bayly because he turned out to be a prolific diary writer and he diarized the whole voyage from start to finish. I was pleasantly surprised when I read Bayly's account of this voyage, because he painted a very positive picture and it seemed that most aboard had a pretty good time.[6]

More about this in the chapter on Richard Edwards and Elizabeth Tumbins/Tomlins

Feb 27th Bayly (p127-8) goes ashore and gives us one of only two first-hand eye witness accounts of the conditions at Clarence Town that we currently have. He describes how many of the settlers appeared to have given up and there was an air of despair, with a lot of them getting drunk every day and lying about in the sand and sun. In contrast to this, on the 28th Feb. he describes how some of the settlers had built themselves very comfortable cottages.

---

[6] "A Life on the Ocean Wave: The Journal of Captain George Bayly 1824-1844" edited Pamela Statham and Ric Erickson Melbourne University Press 1998

The Settlers Gazette (page 6) quotes an early settler Jane Dodd "The town of Clarence appeared more like a gypsy's camp than a town, here a decent tent, there a ragged one, then a half-built mud hut or two. Further on the beach there seemed to be families with no shelter but an awning and green bough to keep off the heat of the sun".[7]

One must sympathize with these early settlers. They had left England with the promise of land grants which never eventuated and the British Govt. had given little thought to providing any infrastructure to assist them in their new land. They really had no idea of the harsh conditions that awaited them and many of them lost most of their possessions either when their boat was wrecked upon landing or in the subsequent fire at Clarence.

A memorial plaque was erected at the site of the Clarence Settlement in 2002. The inscription is etched in a natural stone and reads as follows:

> The Clarence Settlement
> 495 members of Thomas Peel's venture,
> arrived aboard three ships. Gilmore, Hooghly
> and Rockingham between Dec. 1829 and May 1830.
> They set up makeshift camps in primitive
> conditions at Clarence.
> In the first year some 40 settlers died of scurvy, dysentery (and)
> other ailments and 6 from childbirth.
> The majority of the deceased were buried
> in the vicinity and a number later
> re-interred in the old Alma Street Cemetery, Fremantle.

---

[7] Settlers Gazette: Western Australian Genealogical Society: Newsletter of the Swan River Pioneers 1829-1838 Special Interest Group Issue No. 31

> Erected on Foundation Day 1 June 2002
> by the Royal Western Australia Historical Society Inc.
> with contributions from the City of Cockburn.
> Department of Conservation and Land Management
> and Midland Monument Works.

By the end of 1829 there were 1,000 people in the colony. By 1831 one million acres of land had been granted but only 200 acres were under cultivation. Shortages of labour, money and food caused great hardship.[1]

A series of accidents and disasters slowed the progress of the colony. The Challenger and Sulphur both struck rocks while entering Cockburn Sound. The Parmelia ran aground, lost her rudder and damaged the keel. The Marquis of Angelesey was wrecked during a storm. Rumours circulated in London that the Swan River settlement had been abandoned and that the Governor and settlers had been moved to Van Diemans Land (Tasmania). It was eventually established that these rumours were untrue but it all left suspicion and caution in the minds of those in power in England and several ships that were advertised as sailing to the colony, did not proceed with their voyage. Berryman (page 31) states "there can be no doubt that the abrupt cessation in Jan 1830 of the flow of emigrants and capital from Britain had a profound effect on the subsequent development of the Swan River Colony". Western Australia stagnated for the next 20 years. There were about 1,500 settlers in 1832 and less than 5,000 in 1950, just prior to the arrival of convicts to the colony.[8]

It goes without saying that conditions for these early settlers were difficult. They initially were living in tents or any makeshift

---

[8] Swan River Letters Volume 1. Collated and edited by Ian Berryman, Swan River Press 2002

housing they could scrape together. But some of them were obviously of hardy stock and slowly they made a life for themselves and their families. There appears to have been two major problems, one was the distribution of suitable land and the other was the non-existence of labour. The fact that no structures had been put in place prior to the first settlers arriving, plus the difficulties experienced by the settlers in securing suitable farming land, made for much discontent and many hardships. Many left the state, going either to the eastern seaboard or back home. Fortunes were lost and life was hard.

Irwin, in 1835 gives a much more positive picture in his report on the position of the Swan River Settlement which he sent to England. He also makes the point that much of the discontentment arose from people unsuited to be early settlers in a new colony.[9]

There are mixed reports about relations with the indigenous peoples. Irwin[8] gives a whole chapter describing his perceptions of the first peoples of Australia and it seems to me that early contacts were positive and reciprocal but the clash of cultural norms and expectations led to altercations with the disposed indigenous peoples and there was a terrible massacre at Pinjarra. It is reported that there was very little crime amongst the European settlers themselves.

---

[9] "The State and Position of Western Australia: commonly called the Swan River Settlement" by Frederick Chidley Irwin of the H.M. 63rd Regiment; Late Commandant of the troops, and acting Governor of the Colony. London: Simpkin, Marshall and Co., Stationers' Court and J Cross,18, Holborn.

De Burgh[10] gives an interesting chapter entitled "Starting a Farm" where he talks about the 'vee' hut made from bush timber and paperbark as initially servicing some settlers as they established vegetable and grain gardens/crops for their subsistence. Next came homes made from clay/sand and straw bricks with timber felled locally and the roof thatched with rushes from the lakes or thick sheets of paperbark. Often the floors of these early homes were rammed earth. The windows were often made of hessian nailed to a frame and pivoted in the centre. Finally, most of these homes were then white washed with home burnt line stirred into water or skimmed milk. Bourke (page 39) describes early temporary homes of 'wattle and daub' with thatched roofs of weeds or paperbark. The more permanent housing was rammed earth or mud brick.[4]

Despite very slow progress, throughout the first 20 years, the settlers remained adamant that convicts could not be sent to WA. Eventually however, the need for convict labour was acknowledged and the first convicts arrived June 1850 (earlier if you count the Parkhurst Boys, which we will hear about later) and for the next 18 years or so a total of 9,668 male convicts were transported to W.A. No female convicts were ever sent to W.A. The population from 1829 to 1850 was only 5,886. However, between 1850 – 1869 it grew to 22,915.

Now we shall hear about our actual ancestors who arrived as pioneer settlers to this colony.[11]

---

[10] "Neergabby: a history of the Moore River and Lower Gingin Brook" by W.J. de Burgh, Shire of Gingin W..A.1976
[11] "The Story of the Swan District 1843-1938". Rev. Canon Alfred Burton. Muhling, Perth 1938

RICHARD EDWARDS 1777-1850 and ELIZABETH TUMBINS/TOMLINS 1784-1866

Richard and Elizabeth were my great, great, great, grandparents

Richard and Elizabeth were our earliest ancestors to arrive in Western Australia from England. Richard was baptised on the 25th May 1777 at Newent, Gloucestershire, England[12] and his parents were Richard Edwards and Sarah Plummer. The officiating Minister at his baptism was Hub Bower Miles Astman and the church warden was Rob Foly.

Unfortunately, much less is known about Elizabeth prior to her marriage to Richard. Indeed, my mother's early research (Maud Thomas), done well before the internet was operating, had Richard marrying an Elizabeth Powell. A Richard Edwards did indeed marry an Elizabeth Powell in 1801 in the Forest of Dean however some excellent research by Chris O'Sullivan[13] shows that on the marriage record, that this Richard and Elizabeth were widower/widow. Chris goes on to show that another Richard Edwards married an Elizabeth Tumlins in 1804 again in the Forest of Dean, and these were much younger people and purely on the basis of this, the evidence points to them being 'our' Richard and Elizabeth. Further-more however, on the death certificate of son George,[14] his parents were clearly stated as Richard Edwards and

---

[12] Forest of Dean Family History Trust
Transcript Details Record (D70286 Entry No 613 page '6 E363

[13] Chris O'Sullivan 2012 Private research statement by Chris giving proof of Eliz. Name being Tumbins.

[14] Forest of Dean Family History Trust. Transcript Details. Record ID 37019 No. 95

Elizabeth Tumbins, so there is little doubt that it was Elizabeth Tumbin/Tomlin that 'our' Richard married.

There is also considerable confusion over the spelling of Elizabeth's maiden name. On the marriage certificate it is Tumlins, on George's death certificate it is Tumbin. Other researchers who match us DNA wise, have her name as Tomlins. Because I have been unable to find records of her birth, it is assumed at this stage (best guess) that Elizabeth's parents were George Tomlins/Tomblin abt 1758-abt 1832 and Elizabeth Hinder 1753-1836,

The Forest of Dean lies between the rivers Severn and Wye. It has been known to exist since about 8000BC. In the 11th Century the Forest was one of the Royal Hunting Grounds. The Forest did not necessarily belong to the king, but dating back from William the Conqueror this Forest was designated The Royal Forest of Dean and was subject to an elaborate system of Forest law administered by Verderers within the Verderers' Court. The function of this court was primarily the protection of wild life within the forest.[15] The Forest also had huge iron ore reserves and abundance of timber and it was extremely important in the production of iron for hundreds of years. By the late 18th Century, the farmers in the Forest were poverty stricken because they were denied hunting rights and were not allowed to remove timber. During the 19th Century there was a huge demand for iron and steel in England which resulted in a major exploitation of the Forest of Dean's coalfields. Despite having to compete with the mining industry, there appears to have been a strong sense of cultural identity amongst those who lived and farmed in the Forest and they were known as the Foresters. Richard was one of these farmers and it is believed that he owned a property in Clearwell in the Forest.

---

[15] "The Verderers and Forest Laws of Dean" Cyril Hart David & Charles (Publishers) Ltd., South d Devon House Newton Abbott Devon 1971

It was here he must have learned his skills as a market gardener and master brick-maker. It is interesting to see names such as Tibberton and Clearwell on old maps of the Forest. Richard and his son Joshua both used these names for their properties here in W.A.

As stated earlier, Richard married in 1804 at Mitcheldean in the Forest, to Elizabeth Tumlins. The Minister was DE Jones (Curate) and the witnesses were Thomas and Mary Palmer[16]

Richard and Elizabeth had 9 children, all born in the Forest of Dean.

Josiah 1806-1864
Richard 1808-1869
Mary 1810-1853
Dinah 1813-1814
George 1814-1897
Samuel 1817-1905
Dinah 1818-1885
Joshua 1820-1866
Matthew1826-1916

Then in 1829 at age 52 Richard and Elizabeth decided to come to W.A. As already explained, things were tough for farmers in the Forest and as discussed in the Background Section, information was being widely circulated about the attractive deals for free settlers to Western Australia. Richard and Elizabeth signed up to Thomas Peel's expedition. They left behind their eldest son Josiah and their eldest daughter Mary. How hard would that have

---

[16] Forest of Dean Family History Trust Transcript Details Record id 37019 No 95

been – to leave your two children and your grandchildren to go to a new country, never to see them again.

They set sail on the "Hooghly" on Oct 25th 1829 from St Katherine Docks being towed out by the "Dart". The captain was Peter Reeves and the second officer was George Bayly and there were 180 emigrants on board. As already stated, it turns out that George Bayly was a prolific diary writer and we are extremely lucky to have his diarised account of the whole voyage of the Hooghly from England to the Swan River Settlement in 1929-30[17]

The Peel settlers were limited in what they could take to the new land.

Richard and Elizabeth chose to bring their half tester cedar bed with them[6]. This bed remained in the Edwards family until sometime in the 1950's. It was then acquired from the "Greenwood" property by the then owner of the Old Maghony Inn (Daily News 1965). I visited this Inn with my parents in the 1970's and saw this bed with small plaque stating the origins and ownership.

---

[17] "A Life on the Ocean Wave: The Journals of Captain George Bayly" 1824-1844
Edited by Pamela Statham and Rica Erickson. Melbourne University Press 1998

Richard Edwards Bed

Private photo taken in 1970's. The inscription on the bed went as follows:

"Brought to the colony by RICHARD EDWARD (a Peel estate settler) on the ship HOOGLEY, arriving at Fremantle Feb. 15, 1830. On arrival EDWARDS found that the Peel business was a fiasco. He got a position as steward, or manager of HENLEY PARK on the SWAN, owned by MR. MACKIE and CAPT. IRWIN (Military commandant of the colony).

Donated by BERTRAM AND FRED EDWARDS

When I revisited in 2013, the museum at Mahogany Inn was no longer operating. No one seemed to know what happened to the bed. Currently the whereabouts of the bed remains unknown to me.

Life aboard the Hooghly may have been cramped but when I read Bayly's diary,[5] I was surprised at how much fun he records them all having. On pp 117/8 he talks about the passengers all partying on New Years Eve so much so that "…I have never heard so much noise on board of any ship in my life". Bayly notes that on Nov 1st the Captain sent for a man who played the violin, and along with a flute and a drum, a band was formed and about 20 couples 'tripped it on the light fantastic toe" p111. He records how on Dec 2nd how it rained and the passengers were collecting water to wash their clothes and it ended up in a good-humoured water fight. On Xmas Eve they had a sing-a-long with some very amusing recitations. After lights out, some of the passengers continued to sing and drink in the dark and kept it up till midnight. He then goes on to describe how a group of young lads stole various items of clothing from some of the other passengers and hid them which apparently caused much amusement for all. Overall, it seems that they had good weather and a reasonably pleasant journey and this is attested to by one of the other passengers aboard, recounting the voyage in a letter he sent back home to England. Devenish[18] remarks how good the weather was on the journey out "...not more than 4 or 5 wet days...We had an excellent Captain" pp159-160.

Bayly[5] makes an interesting note on Jan 28 (p121) that "Will Edwards fell overboard" and describes how the captain called out to the boy to lie on his back and not be afraid while they lowered the life boats and retrieved him. Later in his diary (p129), he referenced how the "old brickmaker (Edwards) (father of the boy who fell overboard) had built himself a very comfortable cottage at Clarence. So, while we have no record of a Will Edwards as a son of Richard, it probably was one of his other sons who fell overboard. George would have been 15, Samuel 12 and Joshua 9. Devenish[7] (pp159-160) in his letter home, also makes reference to this event and told of a twelve-year old boy who fell overboard during the voyage. So, it was probably Samuel who fell overboard and was rescued. Poor Elizabeth. What shock and trauma that must have caused her. Bayly[5] says that the mother was overwrought and took several days to recover.

By the end of the journey, and as they neared the Western Australia coast, Bayly records how many of the passengers were apprehensive about what they would face in this new land. On Feb 13th 1830 they sighted land.

On Feb 27th Bayly[5] goes shore and gives us one of only two first-hand eye witness account of the conditions at Clarence Town that we have. "Many of the settlers on shore seems to have given themselves up to despair, and a great many, so long as they can procure the means, get drunk every-day and lie about in the sun, so that several have been laid up with the fever. The soil is represented

---

[18] Swan River Letter Volume 1 collected and edited by Ian Berryman, Swan River Press 2002

as being all sandy with the exemption of a few small patches of good land". (p127) He then goes on to write how Edwards (the old brickmaker) "had built a very neat little cabin and thatched it with rushes. It was certainly by far the best I came upon. His wife and family looked clean and respectable and everything wore an air of cheerfulness. He was employed by Mr Peel as a sort of foreman over some workmen. His sons were also employed. The old man had been very careful of his allowance of provisions on the passage out and had saved a considerable quantity of biscuit, beef, port, etc. so that he was better off in that respect than many of those who possessed more ample means of procuring those necessaries, as they were paying an extravagant price for them… He told me he had travelled several miles around in all directions to endeavour to find some earth fit to make bricks but had not as yet succeeded".

So here we have our Richard and Elizabeth already showing their metal and proving their resourcefulness. Conditions at Clarence were terrible and by the end of 1830 most of the people had left to find employment elsewhere. It is interesting to note how Richard is referred to as an old man when in fact he was 52 years of age.

We don't know exactly when Richard left Clarence but we do know that in the first census of Western Australia in 1832,[19] Richard is listed as number 8. He is described as 55 years of age, married a Brickmaker, arrived on the Hooghly. There is also mention that he arrived with Levey. Levey appears to be one of the investors who funded the Peel venture. Elizabeth (Richard's wife), is recorded as number 9 in the census and the children Richard, George, Dinah, Joshua, Samuel and Matthews are listed 10-15 and they are all recorded as living at Henley Park. In total, only 1,233 people were recorded in this first census although this census did not include

---

[19] "A Colony Detailed: The First Census of Western Australia 1832" by Ian Berryman, Creative Research Perth 1979

the people at King George Sound (Albany) and there were 40 people there, Augusta (52) or Murray (5). There were also 5 on Garden Island and 72 in the Canning District. The Survey was ordered by James Stirling who took it to England in the latter part of 1832 hoping to encourage the Colonial Office to take a more active interest in the colony. Berryman goes on to note that whilst about a million acres of land had been set aside, only a few hundred acres had been brought into cultivation by 1832. Stirling was aware of the unfavourable reports that were circulating about the colony and the fact that the principle private financial supporters, Solomon Levey and Peter Lautour were both in financial difficulties. Many settlers had left the colony and many were disgruntled about the quality of the land and Stirling reasoned that the only remedy was to get more financial input and interest from England.

I also have a copy of a handwritten letter from F.C. Irwin[20] to Mr Roe, the Surveyor General, seeking advice as to whether Richard Edwards could obtain a grant of land at Fresh Water Bay, where he had discovered lime-stone. Whilst I cannot find a date on the letter, it would have been at about the same time as the survey.

---

[20] Battye Library Perth Western Australia SDUR/11 13 1830

> Check:
>
> SDUR/I 13 1530, Battye Library
>
> "Perth Tuesday.
>
> Dr Roe,
>
> Old Edwards my brickmaker up The Swan, has discovered some good limestone in Freshwater Bay, about ¾ of a mile I believe from Butler's grant, and he is desirous of getting a grant of the spot, either in his own name, or if his being indentured to Peel would prevent it, to have it granted to me. He says he could supply the community with lime at 10/- per Bushel, which, in the prospect we have of building with stone well be most desirable to secure.
>
> Will - you be good enough to say which should be done to for us.... the object.-
>
> Yours faithfully,
> F. C. Irwin."
>
> Marked on front of letter "Capt. Irwin for a limestone grant for .. Edwards in Freshwater Bay."
>
> Also marked in pencil "Edwards being an indentured servant cannot receive land applied for. Application had better be made in form of a conditional permission to occupy on specified terms & to quit when required."

Irwin's letter re Richard Edwards

Again, we see the initiative displayed by Richard in travelling by boat to find lime for the bricks for Irwin and Mackie's proposed house, which he later built. He found suitable lime-stone at Freshwater Bay.

Irwin[21] describes Richard as 'indefatigable' and 'a man of intelligence and observation'. (p35). Richard was employed for four years by Irwin as manager of Henley Park. Irwin says that as well as having his own trade as a brick and tile maker, Richard was also competent with farming, gardening, bricklaying, lime-burning and brewing. "Such is his industry, that he has been seen working for hours in the garden by moonlight, after spending a long day at labour in the field." (p35) At the same time, Irwin also mentions Elizabeth as a 'regular dairywoman'. Later on in his report, Irwin goes on to devote over two whole pages to describe Richard's accomplishments, which is astonishing really. Astonishing not only in what Richard accomplished, but also that Irwin should spend so much time describing his accomplishments in a general report to England on the state of the Swan River Colony. Pages 57-59 are devoted to describing Richard's accomplishments including the building of a two storied-house at Henley Park, "In the farm-yard he has many ingenious contrivances to meet the wants and habits of its various tribes. His geese and ducks are provided with ample pools, in the sides of which he has constructed dwellings suitable to them, where they find protection from the heat, and security from the native dog… his cattle and pigs are kept in find order". (p 57) In the garden Richard appears to have been also extremely successful. He constructed earthen pipes for irrigation and grew a large variety of vegetables and fruit. "the tomato grows

---

[21] "The State and Position of Western Australia: commonly called the Swan River Settlement" by Captain Frederick Chidley Irwin of H.M. 63rd Regiment: late commandant of the Troops and acting Governor of the Colony. 1835 London: Simpkin, Marshall and Co., Stationers' Court and J. Cross 18 Holborn

here luxuriantly, weighed down with the load of its beautiful fruit, which gives so fine a flavour to sauces, soups etc. Among the fruit-trees, he has raised many hundred almonds and Cape-gooseberries...figs and vines in abundance...".

Irwin makes the point that he has given a much large space than he intended with these details of Richard's accomplishment, 'partly to do justice to a faithful and valuable servant, and principally with a view of conveying some useful instruction to those who may have yet to learn what are the requisites for a successful colonist". (p57)

For all the many descendants of Richard and Elizabeth Edwards, Irwin's report makes very interesting reading and I thoroughly recommend it.

The 1832 Census[22] lists the Edwards family all together in one house. It lists Richard Edwards 55 Brickmaker, Elizabeth 48 his wife, Richard 24 single, carpenter, George 18 brickmaker, Dinah 15, Joshua 12 brickmaker, Samuel 9, Matthew 7.

Richard also built this cottage at Albion Town for William Haddrill in 1834[23]

---

[22] "A Colony Detailed: the first census of Western Australia" 1832 Ian Berryman

[23] Private photo donated to Maud Thomas by Mavis Munro. Mavis being descendant of William Haddrill

Haddrill Cottage ("Albion Town" West Swan. Built 1834 by Richard Edwards. Photo taken around 1895.

In addition to working on his own property E1 which I will discuss later, Richard also built a second two storied home for George Leake. Richard was hired by Lieutenant Bull on behalf of George Leake to build this house which was described as being rivalled only in grandeur by Irwin's House.[24]

In 1834 Richard and his son Richard Jnr were on jury duty as reported in the Perth Gazette and Western Australian Journal 1833-1847 – Saturday 10th May 1834 p282…

The following map was prepared by Mr G.W. Paris, Chief Draughtsman of the Surveyor General's staff, through the courtesy of J.P. Camm Esq., the Surveyor General. Some 1,500 acres known as E1 are listed to R. Edwards whilst G is listed to R.

---

[24] "On the Swan" MJ. Bourke University of Western Australia Press 1987

Edwards (Jnr). Notice the long 'ribbon' blocks stretching from the river to the sea. This was to provide as many people access to the river as possible as the river was a frequent source of transport.[25]

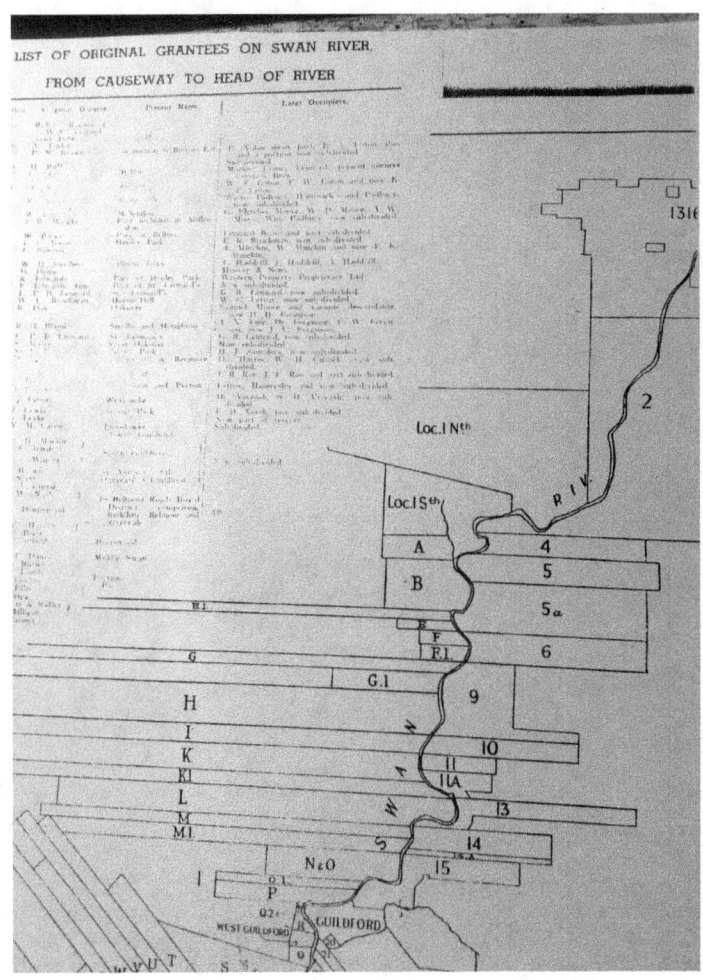

List of Original Grantees on Swan River

---

[25] Map of original holdings on the Swan" G.W. Paris. Perth W.A. Dept. of Land and Survey 1938

As well as achieving all of the above, Richard, at the same time was building his own home on E1 (1,500 acres) which he named "Clearwell". This home was burnt down just prior to Richard's death. After Richard's death, his sons rebuilt the house for their mother and the Edwards family are named as subsequent occupants.

Private photo Edwards House taken 1978

This house still stands today although it is now privately owned and not accessible to the general public. The road no longer runs in front of the house. A small group of descendants of Richard Edwards had a meal together at the restaurant adjacent to the house and the owners were particularly friendly and generous in allowing us to go through the house.

The house is heritage listed and a visit to this web site is well worth it since it provides a good history of the family and house and detailed descriptions of the renovations that have occurred over the years. Further information about this house can be obtained from the Heritage W.A. website.

It is worth reflecting for a moment on all that Richard and Elizabeth achieved. So much history is written about the people in powerful and influential positions and we tend to forget that underneath this is the unrecognized contribution of people like Richard, supported by Elizabeth, who helped establish the colony in major and substantial ways. Without Richard where would Irwin have lived and how would he have survived?

On behalf of the hundreds of descendants from this couple, I salute you Richard and Elizabeth!

Richard Edwards House. Private photo taken 2017

Oh, and I almost forgot, Richard also built the original little church in the Swan Valley. Major Irwin was a devout Anglican and had been holding church services in his home since 1830. When the Anglican Church decided to build a church on the Western side of the river, he and Mackie donated one acre of their land (Location B), for this purpose. Construction of the All Saints Church was commenced by Richard in 1839 who was still Irwin's manager at Henley Park. The church was mainly built with voluntary labour and materials. The bricks were made of local clay. It was opened Jan 10th 1841. It is well worth visiting this little church which is still open. Irwin Mackie and Edwards are all buried in the churchyard.

All Saints Church, Upper Swan. Private picture taken about 1970

It is truly exhausting to think of all that Richard accomplished – and in a relatively short period of time. I think that all the hundreds of people in W.A. who can claim descendancy from him, should be very proud.

The early settlers grew their own vegetables and fruit and shot wildlife for meat. This practice of shooting the wild life was one of the major disputes between the indigenous peoples and the new white settlers. The indigenous peoples were reported to have been friendly initially mainly because they believed that the white people would come and then leave. As time passed and this didn't happen, they would have watched the white settlers shooting their wild turkeys and kangaroos and would probably have resented this. When they, in turn helped themselves to the white settler's food supplies such as vegetables, sheep and poultry etc. they were often fired upon. There were numerous disputes between the two cultures, the most eventful one being the shooting of Yagan, an

Aboriginal leader on the river bank on July 11th 1833. Yagan had a price placed on his head following the murder of two white settlers. Irwin authorized a reward of thirty pounds for his capture, death or alive. (p 4 Perth Gazette 4th May 1833) Yagan and others were known to be raiding the vegetables gardens and were reported to have been seen by Mrs Edwards[26] (page 204).

The December 1837 census of population, stock and crops, lists Richard Edwards as one of nine agricultural farmers in the area with 60 acres of wheat under cultivation and a flock of 200 sheep[27].

Richard was also one of the very early land holders in the Gingin area. In 1844 he applied for 226 acres of land, Location 103 with frontage to the Gingin Brook. This was followed by a further block of 310 acres, Location 113 in Gingin[28]

These blocks of land in Gingin were left to his sons Samuel, Joshua and Matthew in his will. Dated 1849.

The Inquirer, Wednesday 14th Feb 1850 and the Perth Gazette of Friday 8th February 1850 both reported a fire that broke out on Richard Edwards property in Upper Swan. It was described as one of the most destructive bush-fire that had occurred for some years Richard's house and outbuildings were all burnt. Richard at that time was unwell and was confined to his bed and had to be carried out of the house. He died a month later.

---

[26] "Diary of Ten Years of an Early Settler" George fletcher Moore 1978 Univeristy of W.A.Press p204
[27] "On the Swan" Bourke M.J. University of Western Australia Press 1987
[28] "Gingin 1830-1960" by Hazel Udell. Shire of Ginging 1980

Because the colony was struggling due largely to lack of labour, the settlers eventually agreed to the transportation of convicts to the settlement.

In 1850 the first 75 convicts arrived in Fremantle on board the "Scindian" and between 1850-1858, 9,721 male convicts arrived to supplement the shortage of labour in the new colony.

Richard died 19th March 1850 and is buried in the churchyard of the historic All Saints Church, Upper Swan. Elizabeth died 26th April 1866 and is buried at the same place.

Richard and Elizabeth's grave. Private photo abt 1970

In his Will (copy held by me) Richard left "Clearwell" to Elizabeth. Upon her death, it was to be distributed between Joshua, Samuel and Matthew. He left his land in Gingin to these same three sons. This consisted of Location 103 (226 acres) and Location 113 (310 acres), known as Wisewood.

The children of Richard and Elizabeth, whom they married and where they died are as follows:

Josiah 1806-1864	Married	Jane Doward	Died in England
Richard 1808-1869	"	Jane Devlin	Died in Australia
Mary 1810-1853	"	William Voice	Died in England Descendant to N.Z.
Dinah 1813-1814			Died England as a baby
George 1814-1897			Died in Australia
Samuel 1817-1905	"	Charlotte Broome	Died in Australia
Dinah 1818-1885	"	John Foss Tonkin	Died in Australia
Joshua 1820-1866		Emma King	Died in Australia
Matthew 1826-1916		Annie King	Died in Australia

My lineage from Richard Edwards and Elizabeth Tumbins

Matthew Edwards and Annie King
Amy Elizabeth Edwards and William Adams York
Frances Ann Isobel York and Frederick Charles Thomas
Alfred Donald (Don) Thomas and Maud M Pratt

MATTHEW EDWARDS 1825-1916 and ANNE (ANNIE) KING abt 1835-1879

Matthew and Annie were my great great-grandparents.

The Matthew Edwards of Millbank and Greenwood.

Matthew Edwards.
Photo from W.J. de Burgh 1976[29]

---

[29] "Neergabby: a history of the Moore River and Lower Gingin Brook" W.J. de Burgh Shire of Gingin 1976

Matthew arrived in Western Australia with his parent Richard and Elizabeth Edwards aboard the "Hooghly" in 1830. He was four years of age. Matthew was born in Gloucestershire, England and was baptised on the 24 June 1825.[30] The Edward's family residence at the time of Matthew's baptism, is stated as Staunton Lane. The officiating minister at the baptism was Alfred Schelding. Matthew's father, Richard, was described as a Brick Maker.

Annie King was born about 1835 in Sydenham, Oxfordshire, England and at the moment of writing no official documentation of her birth has been found. Her birth date has been calculated from her death certificate and the 1841 English Census. Ann's parents were Richard (Constant) King and Elizabeth Anne Gardiner. I have been unable to find a record of Richard and Elizabeth's arrival in Western Australia, but Hazel Udell[31] states that the death certificate of their daughter Emma (who married Joshua Edwards), indicates that they probably arrived in 1844 aboard the "Trusty".

Matthew is recorded in the Australian School Indexes 1830-1970[32] as being a student at Clarence. Then again in the 1832 Census[33] he is recorded as being 7 years of age and living with his parents and siblings.

De Burgh[1] suggests that the Edward brothers, Matthew and Joshua were grazing stock along the lower parts of the Gingin Brook and Moore River by the early 1850's. They appear to have

---

[30] Forest of Dean Family History Trust Transcript of Parish Records Record ID 83802 Entry 337
[31] "Gingin 1830-1960" by Hazel Udell, 1980 Gingin Shire Council W.A.
[32] Rockingham, Western Australia, Australia School Indexes 1830-1970
[33] "A Colony Detailed; the first census of Western Australia" 1832 Edited by Ian Berryman

had two properties, Millbank and Greenwood. In March 1852 the lease at Millbank was increased to 12,000 acres.[1]

Matthew and Ann married on the 5th January 1853[34] at Middle Swan. It is reported by de Burgh,[1] that Matthew was the first settler to marry in the area. Matthew and Ann lived at Millbank where they established a substantial home which they built in 1853. They also built a horse driven flour mill and a small cottage on the south side of the main house. This cottage became the home of John and Catherine Christian who worked for Matthew.[1]

The flour mill at Millbank was working during the 1860's. There were two flour mills in the district, one at Cowalla one and one at Millbank. The mill at Cowalla was driven by a water wheel and it was known to be working in 1859. P 39. It is rumoured that the Cowalla mill was destroyed by floods in 1862 and for the next ten years wheat was carted from Cowalla to Millbank for grinding.[1]

Apparently in 1872 floods damaged the flour mill at Millbank which was repaired and it operated for a further couple of years until one day the horses smashed the whole thing up. Matthew and Anne lived at Millbank until 1894 when they retired. From 1919 Millbank was unoccupied apart from when some of the Edwards children camped there during the week in order to attend school. All this information comes from de Burgh's book.[1] As late as 1976 Matthews' great grandsons still owned Millbank. The ruins of Millbank house are registered with inherit, the State Heritage Register and this web site can easily be accessed for free. Even though it was registered as of heritage value, Millbank was classified at the lowest level of Category 3 which meant that no restrictions or conditions were required for maintenance.

---

[34] Australian Marriage Index 1788-1950 Ancestry.com.au

In 2012 myself and my two siblings set out to explore the Moore River area with the aim of finding the Millbank ruins. At the end of Millbank Road, we found that the area had been subdivided into a housing estate selling five-acre blocks. On one of these blocks, were the ruins of Millbank House.[35]

Millbank ruins.

As I stood looking at the ruins, I felt a profound sense of sadness as I thought of the hardships of isolation and limited transportation these pioneers experienced as they built their homes and cleared the land for grazing and planting. They worked hard and raised large families in relatively small homes. It is on the back of these strong resilient pioneer people, that our current communities were largely built yet we have carelessly allowed the only evidence of the lives of these two, ordinary people, to decay and be destroyed.

---

[35] Personal photo taken 2012

I have not been back to this site since 2012 as I fear what I might find.

In about 1858 Matthew built a further house, this time on the Greenwood property which he also managed. Edward and Mary Larwood worked for Matthew and lived there.[5]

The current Greenwood house was built in 1886 by Herbert Edwards, the second son of Matthew.[1] Fortunately it has been lovingly restored by people over the years and thus preserved for posterity. In 2017 when all 'the cousins' visited Greenwood, it was a well renovated and loved home. The then occupants were very generous in allowing us all to troop through their home. Greenwood is listed with inherit as a State Heritage home site 11790[36].

The current owners of the Greenwood property are Graham and Cathy Walton and they have graciously given me permission to use my photos of their house. They spoke lovingly of the house and property and are intent on preserving it for their later generations to enjoy. It is very reassuring that this house and property is in such capable and loving hands and will be preserved.

---

[36] "inherit" Western Australia State Heritage Register

'old' Greenwood House

'old' Greenwood House

The above two private photos were taken in 1977 and since then the house has been restored and renovated.

Greenwood 2017

Greenwood 2017

Greenwood 2017

These last three private photos of Greenwood were taken in 2017.

So, we can see that Matthew inherited his father's skills and energy levels. He achieved a lot in his long life. There is a small island off the WA coast named Edward Island, just north of Ledge Point. This is shown and talked about by de Burgh in his book "Story of the Cowalla Coast Run 1873-1964" (p8,9 and 10).

In 1879 Ann died[37] and by 1903 Matthew was living in James St., Perth and listed as a 'prospector'[38]. Further Electoral Rolls in 1906 show Matthew still living in James St and again listed as a 'prospector'. In the 1910 Electoral Roll Matthew is living at 27 Mary St., North Perth and his occupation is given as a 'gentleman' He was by then 85 years old.

---

[37] Australian Death Index 1787-1985 (Ancestry.com)
[38] Australian electoral Rolls 1903-1980 (Ancestry.com)_

June 6th 1916 Matthew died. At the time he was living at 425 Rokeby Rd., Subiaco[39]. de Burgh states that at the time Matthew was living with his two unmarried daughters Julie and Annie.

Matthew is buried at Karrakatta Cemetery, Western Australia[40]

Children of Matthew and Ann

Amy Elizabeth	1854-1922	m	William Adams York	1856-1933
Arthur J	1857-1945	m	Fanny Woolhouse	1862-1938
Frederick William	1859-1915			
Herbert Matthew	1860-1942	m	Mary Anne Edwards	1867-1898
Priscilla Matilda	1861			
Charles Augustus	1863-1865		died young	
Julie Aileen	1864-1935		never married	
Florence Amelia	1865-1952	m	Hugh John Thomas	1865-1948
Edith Maud	1867-1948	m	Thomas Richard Darch	
Anne	1868-1951		never married	
Laura Gardiner	1870-1941	m	Francis John Darch	1869-1950
Ernest	1872-1874		died young	

My Lineage from Matthew and Ann
Amy Elizabeth Edwards and William Adams York
Frances Ann Isobel York and Frederick Charles Thomas
Alfred Donald (Don) Thomas and Maud M Pratt

---

[39] Australian death Index 1787-1985 (Ancestry.com.au) and Copy of death certificate.
[40] Australia and New Zealand, Find a Grave Index, 1800s-Current

JOHN YORK 1812-1896
and
ANN ADAMS 1811-1897

John York and Ann Adams were my great, great, grandparents.

John York and Ann Adams

Photo from 'Gingin 1830-1960" by Hazel Udell 1979 Gingin Shire Council, W.A.p66

John and Ann arrived in W.A. in 1842 and settled in Gingin as graziers and farmers.

John was born on the 20th Nov. 1812 in Northamptonshire, England.[41] There is an earlier baptism recorded for a John with the same parents in 1811 so it is probable that the first child died as a baby and when the next child was born a year later and was also a boy, he was also called John. His parents were William York and Sarah Baker. William was a weaver.

Northamptonshire is a land locked county in the centre of England. In 1823 it was said to enjoy 'a very pure and wholesome air' and in 1832 it was described as 'a county enjoying the reputation of being one of the healthiest and pleasant parts of England'. It was often referred to as the county of 'spire and squires' because of the large numbers of stately homes and ancient churches. From about 1850 Northamptonshire became more industrialized. It became the boot and shoe making capital of the world and eventually established a major steel industry.[42]

Ann was baptised 27th October 1811 in Spratton, Northamptonshire, England.[43] Her parents were William Adams and Ann Francis. To-date no documented evidence of her birth has been found.

John and Ann were married 14th November 1833 in Spratton, Northamptonshire, England.[44]

In the 1841 English Census of the parish of Great Creaton, Northamptonshire, John York is recorded as 25 years of age, and Ann as 30. This discrepancy can, I believe, be explained by the custom of rounding down ages to the lower multiple of 5. John

---

[41] Northamptonshire, England, Church of England Baptisms, 1813-1912
[42] Wikipedia – Northamptonshire, England
[43] Northamptonshire, England Church of England Baptisms, Marriages, Burials 1532-1812 (Ancestry)
[44] England, Select Marriages 1538-1973 (Ancestry)

would have been 29 in 1841 and following the 'rounding down' custom, they would have put him at 25. Frances was 5, Selina 3 and Emma 1.[45]

In the early 1840's John Hutt, Governor of Western Australia sent 3,500 pounds to Britain to provide assisted passage for migrants to bolster the workforce in the new colony of W.A. Presumably this was the incentive for John and Ann to come to W.A.

John and Ann left London aboard the "Simon Taylor" on the 30th April 1842 and arrived in Fremantle 20th August 1842. John and Ann and their three eldest daughters travelled with John's brother Joseph, his wife Mary and their two children.[46]

The Simon Taylor was a barque used to transport assisted migrants to W.A. A barque is a type of sailing vessel with three or more masts having the fore and mainmasts rigged square. Most ocean-going vessels were four-mastered barques, since the four masted barque is considered the most efficient rig available largely because of the ease of handling. The Simon Taylor was built in 1824 for Meek and co., and was constructed at the Blackwall Yard on the River Thames in London. It weighed 431 tons and the passenger deck was 140 feet long with a height of 7 foot 6 inches between decks. The captain was Thomas Brown and the Surgeon Superintendent was Mr Cooper. Mr Cooper received free cabin passage and 10 shillings per head for each immigrant who landed safely in the colony. For the April to August voyage to W.A. there were 141 adults (82 males and 59 females), 34 children between the ages of 7 and 14 years and a further 44 children under the age of 7 years and a crew of 26. Amongst the passengers were 18

---

[45] 1841 English census (Ancestry)
[46] Passenger Ships arriving in Western Australia "Simon Taylor" Aug 20 1842

Parkhurst apprentices or juvenile offenders from the Isle of Wight sent out to W.A. as indentured apprentices.[47]

John and Joseph initially took their families to Newcastle (Toodyay) and worked on the Culham property for an S.P. Phillips.[48]

In 1845 John and Joseph moved to Gingin and leased Swan Location 96 from W.L. Brockman for 95 pounds. Joseph later sold his share of this land to his brother for 50 pounds and moved to Northam. Udell states that it is likely that John built the original cottage on Swan Location 96. In 1849 John bought Swan Location 115 (30 acres) and this is where he built his home which he called Creaton.

In 2017 a group of cousins all descendants from John and Ann York did a weekend trip to Gingin to find and record the old historic home sites of our ancestors. We found Creaton or rather we found where Creaton had been, which was Lot 115 Creighton Rd., Breera. Below a diagrammatic depiction of the Creaton farm in 1880[8] (page 59)

---

[47] Wikipedia
[48] "Gingin 1830 to 1960" Hazel Udell Gingin Shire Council 1979

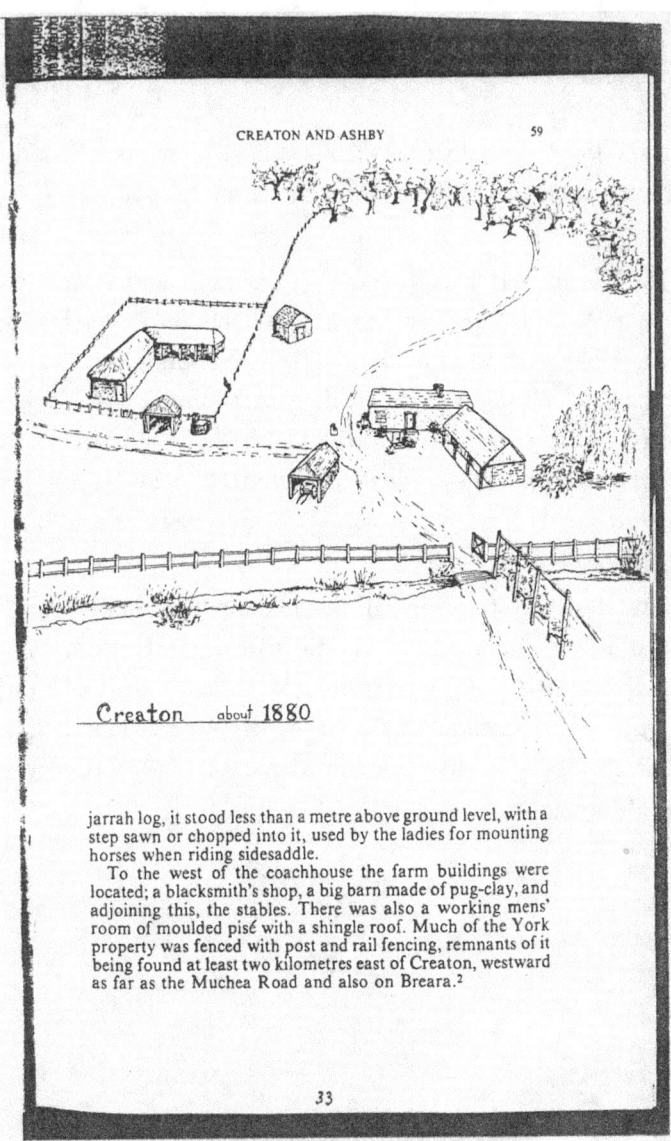

jarrah log, it stood less than a metre above ground level, with a step sawn or chopped into it, used by the ladies for mounting horses when riding sidesaddle.

To the west of the coachhouse the farm buildings were located; a blacksmith's shop, a big barn made of pug-clay, and adjoining this, the stables. There was also a working mens' room of moulded pisé with a shingle roof. Much of the York property was fenced with post and rail fencing, remnants of it being found at least two kilometres east of Creaton, westward as far as the Muchea Road and also on Breara.[2]

Creaton Farm 1880

Creaton is now a privately owned property. The owners were extremely friendly and generously allowed us onto their property to see the site of the original house. According to the current owners, a fire in 1916 burnt down the remains of the original house. All that remains now is the old coach shed which the current owner has lovingly restored. There are also some house and fruit trees that show where the original house had been located. Below are two photos taken by me of the restored coach house which give an excellent view of the stone work which would have been done by John. When describing Creaton, Udell states that the fireplace featured a Yorkshire flagstone of about 120cms in length and 40cms wide which was brought from England by John and was part of the ballast in the sailing ship Simon Taylor. Udell states that in 1979 this stone was in the possession of K.E. Dewar who at the time owned Creaton. I wonder where it is now?

Old Coach shed at Creaton

Private photo of the old stone coach shed built originally by John York and restored by the current owners.

According to notes on the York family by Udell,[49] John built four houses in Gingin, Spratton, Breara, Hillview and Creaton. Udell also goes on to point out that John's son John York Jnr was the first white child born at Gingin on Oct 13, 1845.

We, 'the cousins' also set off to find Spratton which is listed as 45 Lennards Rd Gingin. This was also one of John York's homes. We had a lot of trouble finding this one but eventually located it in the middle of a commercial orchard to which we had no access. Verbal reports of neighbours said it was an old, derelict house which during winter stands in water. The Orchard is owned by Westralian Farm Fruits. Another sad story of an historic house left to go to ruins.

A survey map of 1860 shows John leased 75,210 acres in the area. Between 1860 and 1870 he purchased many blocks of land including Swan Locations 338, 344, 345, 346, 369, 407, 415 and 443. He also bought Locations 108 and 109 from George Fletcher Moore in 1852. He also purchased Locations 449, 450, 451, 466 and 521. What a busy lad he was![8] Udell states that the family lost much of this land when the Midland Railway Company took over the land in the 1980's.

In 1846 John, along with his brother Joseph and Samuel Mortimore, placed an advertisement in the Inquirer[50] stating that twelve months ago, one black steer and one red heifer, both about 2 years old had strayed onto their property at Creaton. Then on 15th September 1847 the same advertisement was again placed in the Inquirer.

---

[49] "The York Familly of Gingin" W.A. State Library PR 14514/YOR/1 notes by Hazel Udell
[50] "Inquirer" 23 December 1846

In 1849, it was stated that at the Quarter Sessions on January 3rd 1849, before W.M. Mackie, that Wawjal, an indigenous Australian man, was found guilty of stealing a goat from the property of John York and sentenced to 7 years transportation.[51] I suspect, (but don't know for sure) that he may have been transported to Rottnest Island.

John was known to be an industrious and hard-working man. He is known to have been literate and played an important role in community affairs. He acted as honorary Postmaster in Gingin 1856-1863 and also as the District Registrar from 1856-1880.[52]

I have a copy of a handwritten letter from John to his son and daughter dated 26th Dec 1884 where he talks about him and Ann having a very nice turkey dinner with a neighbour and Ann getting violently ill after this with 'hives'.

John died 11th April 1896 aged 83.[53] Ann died 5th March 1897.[54] A copy of his death certificate states the cause of death as 'rupture and natural decay'. A newspaper death notice states that he left 72 Grand Children and 72 Great Grand Children!! Both are buried at Gingin.

---

[51] Perth Gazette and Independent Journal of Politics and News (WA 1848-1864) 6th January 1849
[52] "The York Family of Gingin" W.A. State Library PR 14514/YOR/1
[53] W.A. Death Certificates
[54] Australian Death Index

Gravestone in Gingin for John and Ann York. Private photo.

John and Ann had the following children"

Francis York	1834-1894	married Joseph Purser
Selena York	1839-1917	married John Dewer
Emma York	1841-1930	married William Smart Dewer
John York	1845-1903	married Harriett Maria McHard
Sarah Ann York	1848-1875	married Robert Quinn *
Elizabeth York	1850-1940	married Alexander Buckingham
Martha York	1854-1895	married Robert Quinn *
William Adams York	1856-1933	married Amy Elizabeth Edwards

- Robert Quinn's first wife Sarah Ann York died at 27 years of age and he then married her sister Martha York

My lineage from John York and Ann Adams
William Adams York married Amy Elizabeth Edwards
Francis Ann Isobel York married Frederick Charles Thomas
Alfred Donald (Don) Thomas married Maud M Pratt

RICHARD (CONSTANT) KING 1799-1891
and
ELIZABETH ANNE GARDINER 1806-1883
(Was known as Ann)

Richard and Ann were my Great, great, great, Grandparents. (Unfortunately – no photo).

Richard was christened on the 8th April 1799 in Sydenham, Oxfordshire, England. His parents were William King and Sarah Taylor.[55]

Sydenham is a small village in the South East of Oxfordshire. Oxfordshire is a landlocked county in South East England. Sydenham has a long history dating back to before the Norman conquest of England (1066). In 1086 the population of Sydenham was 26. Sydenham had always been dependent on agriculture. In the early 19th Century, most of Sydenham was owned by one or two wealthy land lords who had tenant farmers on their land. Because of the almost total dependence on agriculture, during difficult years or when crops failed, there was wide spread poverty. This led to many families emigrating. Things were so bad in 1851 that the census of that year, described many of the labourers of this district as paupers.[56]

---

[55] Oxfordshire, England, Church of England Baptists, Marriages and Burials 1538-1812
Sydenham 1788-1812 (Ancestry.com)

[56] Wikipaedia

Ann was baptised on the 9th March 1806 at Brize, Norton, Oxfordshire, England. Her parents were Joseph and Mary Gardiner. Mary's maiden name is unknown at this point in time.[57]

Richard and Ann were married on the 6th March 1823 at Aston, Rowant, Oxford, England.[58]

In the English Census of 1841, Richard and Ann are recorded as being 40 and 30 years of age respectively (remember the rounding down system whereby ages were rounded down to the lower multiple of 5 in this census). They were living Thame, Sydenham, Oxfordshire. Emma was 12, Daniel 9, Ann 7, Elizabeth 4 and Eliza was 1.[59]

Richard owned a Manchester and warehousing business.[60]

There is no record of their arrival in Western Australia but Hazel Udell[61] states that on the death certificate of their daughter Emma (Anderson), it indicates that they came in 1844.

Pamela Statham records that Richard received goods from England on the "Unicorn" in 1844. (p187)[62]

---

[57] Oxfordshire, England, Church of England Baptisms, Marriages and Burials 1538-1812
Brize Norton 1756-1812 (Ancestry.com)
[58] England, Select Marriages, 1538-1973 (Ancestry.com)
[59] 1841 England Census (Ancestry.com.au)
[60] "Neergabby a history of the Moore River and Lower Gingin Brook 1830-1960" W.J. de Burgh 1976 Shire of Gingin.
[61] "Gingin 1830-1960" by Hazel Udell, 1979 Shire of Gingin
[62] "Dictionary of Western Australians 1829-1914 Vol 1, Pamela Statham, 1979 University of WA Press 1979

In 1860 Richard and Ann are known to have been in Gingin as Farmers & Graziers and Richard qualified as a juror in that same year. (P469)[63]

To-date I have found little about Richard and Ann and I do not know where they lived, although their children certainly feature prominently in the early history of Gingin. Daniel King was granted 4,000 acres situated where the Mungala and Gingin brooks meet and he called his property Mount Pleasant. Anne of course married our Matthew Edwards and lived at Millbank. Emma married Joshua Edwards and they lived at Tibberton in the township of Gingin.

Ann died in 1883 and William died in 1891[64]

CHILDREN OF RICHARD AND ANN KING

Priscilla King	1825-1883	m	George Woolhouse	1819-1900
Emma	1828-1901	m	Joshua Edwards	1820-1866
Daniel	1832-1890	m	Ann Mortimer	
Annie	1835-1879	m	Matthew Edwards	1825-1916
Elizabeth	1836-1905	m	Francis Leitch Hussey	1835-1909
Eliza	1839-1905			
William Thomas	1842-1931	m	Selena Clara Lazenby	1842-1900

My Lineage from William and Ann King
Anne King and Matthew Edwards
Amy Elizabeth Edwards and William Adams York
Frances Ann Isobel York and Frederick Charles Thomas
Alfred Donald (Don) Thomas and Maud M Pratt

---

[63] "Dictionary of Western Australians 1829-1914 Vol 3 Rica Erickson, 1979 University of WA Press
[64] Australian Death Index, 1787-1985 – Ancestry.com.au

JOHN THOMAS 1829-1920
and
MARIA BUCKINGHAM 1836-1919

John Thomas and Maria Buckingham were my great grandparents.[65]

John Thomas and Maria Buckingham

---

[65] Picture from "Neergabby: a history of the Moore River and Lower Gingin Brook" by W.J. de Burgh 1976 Shire of Gingin Western Australia

Our next arrival from England to Western Australia did not come voluntarily. John was a juvenile offender and was sent to Western Australia as part of what has become known as the "Parkhurst Boys" plan. More about this later.

John Thomas was born 1829 in Ramsgate Kent, England. His parents were John Henry Thomas and Ann Matilda Pampflett. John was christened on the 5th June 1831 at St George's in Ramsgate, Kent England.[66]

Ramsgate us a seaside town in the district of Thanet in East Kent, England. It is in the parish of St Lawrence. It was one of the great English seaside towns of the 19th Century. Originally Ramsgate was a small fishing village but in the second half of the 17th Century, a harbour was constructed and by the 19th Century, Ramsgate became a major seat of sea trade and travel for England.

Maria was Baptised on the 23rd October 1836 in Devon, England[1]. Her parents were Thomas Buckingham and Mary Chanter. According to the records of Thomas and Mary's wedding, the Buckinghams lived in North Molton which is an ancient market town on the river Mole. Maria (not to be confused with her sister Mary), arrived in Western Australia aged 13, with her parents aboard the "Sophia". (more about this in the chapter about her parents Thomas Buckingham and Mary Chanter).

On the 28th January 1845 at 15 years of age, John was convicted of larceny and sentenced to 3 months imprisonment.[67]

---

[66] England, births and Christenings 1538-1975 (Ancestry.com.au)
[67] England & Wales, Criminal Registers 1791-1892 (Ancestry.com.au)

Then on the 18th November 1845 at Middlesex, England, when he is 16 years of age, John was convicted of stealing bread and sentenced to seven years transportation.[2]

On the 7th January 1846 John, still aged 16, was received at Parkhurst prison from Millbank prison. He was discharged from Parkhurst prison on the 19th Oct 1848 to be transported to Western Australia where he was to be apprenticed[68] p45

Between 1842-1849 two hundred and thirty- four juvenile convicts aged between 10-20 years were sent from Parkhurst prison on the Isle of Wight, England, to Western Australia. Once in the colony, they were 'pardoned' on two conditions – that they were apprenticed to local employers and that they did not return to the country in which they had been convicted.

Gill[3] states that by far the greatest number of Parkhurst Boys sent to Western Australia between 1842-49 were convicted of larceny (theft) and had been sentenced to 7 years transportation. The greatest majority were between 16-18 years with one being only 10 years of age. Thirty eight percent of these boys were listed as being able to read and write 'imperfectly" and nineteen percent could do both well. pp24-5

Gill[3] argues strongly that the Parkhurst Boys were convicts just like any other convicts transported to Australia. However, they were never recognized as convicts in WA. Presumably because Western Australia had been settled on the basis that there were to be no convicts sent there. All these boys were pardoned upon arrival in WA and apprenticed to local employers.

---

[68] "A Register of Parkhurst Convicts 'apprenticed' in Western Australia 1842-18551" by Andrew Gill, Perth Western Australia 1992

John arrived in W.A. on the "Ameer" on February 1849 and was apprenticed to a R Waters between 1849-1851. It was written of John 'a very good lad' "Thomas is a rather superior lad but early in the half year he had several disagreements with his master. Latterly they have got on well together". 'Has been imprisoned 2 months for misconduct – but his general character is good'.³ p45

What a traumatic early childhood experience for John. It is interesting to speculate as to why a young lad who could read and write and seemingly came from a good family, took to a life of crime so young. I use the term 'seemingly came from a good family', because on John's death certificate, his father was cited as being a Customs Officer. John had an older brother Charles and on Charles's death certificate, the father was cited as a Naval Officer. So, either way, John's father was obviously educated and literate and so one could expect that he would have been able to provide adequately for his family. Unfortunately, I have been unable to find much about John Snr so perhaps he died when our John was very young and left the family destitute or maybe he was is prison. At this stage, we just don't know. We know that John's mother was Ann Pampflett because of numerous DNA matches along this line.

It is not known where John was after 1851 but de Burgh in his book "Neergabby"⁶⁹ states that John was living with Maria and Edward Bentley at Wannerie in 1958, probably as a farm assistant. Edward drowned in the Karakin Brook on the 2ⁿᵈ September 1859⁴ leaving Maria with a very small child, Levi.

---

[69] "Neergabby: s history of the Moore River and Lower Gingin Brook" by W.J. de Burgh 1976 shire of Gingin

John and Maria Bentley nee Buckingham were married in Gingin on the 16th Jan 1861.[4] Theirs was the first marriage to be held in the new St Luke's Church, Gingin, W.A. The ceremony was conducted by Rev George Bostoch.[70] John and Maria continued to farm at Wannerie and raised a large family until Maria died in 1919 and John in 1920.

De Burgh[4] talks about how Maria used to ride from Wannerie to Roleystone on a horse, to visit her mother. It is reported that one day she carried a swarm of bees tied up in a pillow case, back to Wannerie on her horse. He also relates how the day before she died, she drove by herself across to Bidaminna to see her daughter-in-law. What a woman!

John was a member of the Gingin Road Board between 1910-1912[71]. John was always described within the family as a man of mystery. A grand-daughter who used to spend school holidays at Wannerie with John and Maria, told a story to my parents of how a stranger once knocked on the door at Wannerie saying that he was trying to locate his brother. Apparently, John refused to see him. We have subsequently found that John had an older brother Charles who was transported to New South Wales as a teenage offender, so it may well have been Charles trying to re-unite with his younger brother. It may be that John's air of mystery relates to the fact that he came to W.A. as a juvenile offender but because all such boys were pardoned on arrived, he is not recorded in the convict records and had no desire to be so identified.

On one of our family's camping excursions, we discovered a well named Thomas Well and de Burgh[72] p8 makes mention of this.

---

[70] Australian Marriage Index 1788-1950 Ancestry.com.au
[71] "Gingin" 1830-1960" by Hazel Udell, '979 Shire of Gingin
[72] "A Story of the Cowalla Coast Run 1873-1964" by WJ. de Burgh

Wannerie which turned out to be the Thomas ancestral home was initially granted as a pastoral lease of 10,000 acres to G. and E. Whitfield. On the western side it joined Matthew Edward's Millbank lease. The land was transferred to Edward Bentley in April 1858. Upon Edward's death it went to Maria.

In the early 1900 Alex and Albert, two bachelor sons of Maria and John, were living at Wannerie with their parents. They had also purchased the original Cockram property, Warren Warren. In 1930 the two brothers were still living at Wannerie but by 1949 Alex had sold Warren Warren to R.M.B. Edwards and sons. Alex died in 1951 and soon after this Alberts health failed and he retired to Perth. Wannerie was sold to J.L.B. Weir of Perth and so ended ninety years of Thomas's at Wannerie. In 1953 Wannerie was purchased by R.H. Jones and considerable improvements were made to the house and new sheds were built.[73]

Wannerie Homestead circa 1900 - Home of Phil's G. Grandparents and grandfather - Frederick Thomas

Wannerie circa 1900

Picture taken from "Neergabby..."[1]

Note the large tree in right hand background. It features in the following photo.

---
[73] "Gingin" 1830-1960" by Hazel Udell 1979 Shire of Gingin

By 2013 when I visited the site, there was nothing left of the house or sheds and the current owner admitted to having bulldozed the remains and buried them.

Wannerie site 2017 Private photo

Directions to find the site of the old Wannerie homestead are as follows: Travel along Gingin road which runs between the Brand Highway and the Indian Ocean Rd., turn left off Gingin Road into Cowala Road. Travel along Cowala road till you come to a small road called Wanerie Road. At the bottom of Wanerie Road, you run into a paddock with two large trees. The old homestead stood next to these two trees. These directions were accurate in 2013 but with all the new housing developments, I cannot guarantee the roads haven't changed.

Maria died in 1919[74] and John died the following year in 1920[9]. At the time of his death John was living in Green St., Osborne Park. Both are buried at St Lukes in Gingin.

Children of John Thomas and Maria Buckingham

Eliza	1861-1919	Unmarried	
Henry Edward	1863-1921	married	Laura Roe
Hugh John	1865-1948	married	Florence Edwards
Alice	1867-1934	married	John Buckingham
Alexander	1869-1951	unmarried	
Anne	1872-1872		
Frederick Charles	1873-1938	married	Frances York
Albert	1875-1949	unmarried	
Flora	1877-1945	married	Herbert Edwards

My Lineage from John Thomas and Maria Buckingham

Frederick Charles Thomas 1873-1938 and Frances Ann Isobel York 1877-1951

Alfred Donald (Don) Thomas 1919- and Maud Mary Pratt 1919 -

---

[74] Australian Death Index 1787-1985 ancestry.com.au

THOMAS BUCKINGHAM 1808-1879
and
MARY CHANTER 1814-1875

Finally, we get to our last ancestors who came from England to Western Australia.

Thomas Buckingham and Mary Chanter were my great, great-grandparents.

The Buckinghams were a large family and there are many descendants actively researching this family. The name is also extremely common – you wouldn't believe how many Thomas Buckinghams there were/are. This makes it difficult to keep track of who is who and to make sure that you have the correct person.

Thomas was born in 1808 in Twitchen, North Devonshire, England. His parents were Thomas Buckingham and Lucretia Hammett. No actual documentation of this found as yet but they are recorded in the Dictionary of Western Australians 1829-1914.[75]

Devonshire is a county of England. It reaches from the Bristol Channel in the north to the English channel in the south. By far the most valuable economic activity in Devon is agriculture and we know that Thomas Buckingham was a farmer in North Devonshire.[76]

---

[75] Dictionary of Western Australians 1829-1914 Volume 3 Free 1850-1868" Rica Erickson 1979 University of Western Australia Press.
[76] Wikipedia

Mary was Christened on the 9th Jan 1814 at North Molton, England.[77] Her parents were John Chanter and Catharine Treble. North Molton is a village in North Devon

Thomas and Mary's eldest son, Thomas (Jnr) wrote his memoirs which are fascinating to read.[78] He talks about how bad things were in England in the 1840's and how there were agents trying to encourage people to go to Australia. The family sold up everything and with 3 waggons to take 3 families, they went forth to Plymouth which was about 70 miles from where they had been living. The three families were "Uncle John Buckingham and Uncle Richard Cockram and their families plus Thomas and Mary and their family" (p2). Thomas Jnr also talks about how they lived on Mongers Lake which is of particular interest to me because that is close to Herdsman Lake, where I was born and lived until I was 20 years of age. He also talked about the fun he had boating and swimming in the lake. It was from here that they went to Leeders farm and then onto the Pinjar in Wanneroo. From Wanneroo Thomas Jnr tells how his father and uncle cut a road through from Wanneroo to

Gingin to build pug houses and barns for settlers. He states that they only stayed at Pinjar about a year and then went onto Gingin where they rented a small pug cottage from Mr Edwards and then went on to lease Moraba for 5 years at 50 pounds per year. He talks of his sister Maria's wedding to Mr Bentley and how everyone in the district was there. Here we get a date for when the family moved to Roleystone as Thomas Jnr says that in 1860 they started shifting their things to the Canning. I will digress here for an interesting snippet when Thomas Jnr tells of his ride down to the Vasse to inspect a saw mill. He rode his horse all the way from

---

[77] England, Select Birth and Christenings 1538-1975 (Ancestry.com.au)
[78] Memoirs of Thomas Buckingham

Kelmscott to Busselton and on the way back he found a body of a man near the river. Thomas says that Moondyne Joe (Joseph Jones) and he made a coffin and buried the man on the river bank with a Mr Cronin reading the burial service.

The first 'solid' evidence that I have is that of Thomas, Mary and their family arriving in Western Australia on the Sophia on the 27 July 1850. The Sophia was a 537 ton, teak and yellow metal ship built in India in 1819. On this particular voyage to W.A., the Captain was John Claborn with William Reid as 1st mate. The Surgeon was Thomas Parr, the Schoolmaster was George Pope, the Hospital assistant was Stephen Donnelly and John Johnson was the constable on board. There were 250 passengers and a crew of 33. The passenger list shows Thomas and Mary with Maria (13 yrs), Thomas Jnr (10) Mary (9), Alexander (6), Betsy (3), Caroline (infant).[79]

Erickson[80] lists the family as 'Buckingham Thomas, b. 1808 (England), son of Thomas & Lucretia. Arrived per "Sophia" 27.7.1850 with family & relative Cockrams. First married (England) 23.10.1835 Mary Chaunter b 1815 (England) d. 21.5.1875. Second married 1877 Mary Plackett. Children" Maria b 1836 d.1919, Thomas b 1839 d.1913, Mary b 1841, Alexander b 1843 d.1897, Betsy b 1846 d.1925, Caroline b 1839 d 1915, Jan b1852 d 1852, William b 1853 d. 1917, Ellen b 1856 d 1878, John b1859 d 1947, Hugh James b 1860 d 1940. Farmer Waneroo & Roleystone: leased Leeder's farm, Perth 1852 to Waneroo then Gingin: sold out to buy 5559 acres at Roleystone in 1858; cattle died of poison; timber milling 1861; sons built water mill". P87

---

[79] Passenger Ships Arriving in Western Australia – Sophia July 27, 1850" Internet

[80] Dictionary of Western Australians 1829-1914 Vol 3 Free 1850-1868" Rica Erickson 1979 University of W.A. Press

De burgh[81] mentions that Thomas and Mary first leased Leeder's farm which was situated between Perth and Monger's Lake for a year of so till they secured a 6,000 acre lease at Lake Bindiar which is about 25 miles north of Joondalup. A relative Richard Cockram and his family joined them there. At Lake Bindiar, de Burgh says they lived in paperbark houses and then both families moved to Gingin.

According to Thomas (jnr) memoirs[4] when they first arrived at Gingin, they rented a cottage from Mr Joshua Edwards. Thomas Buckingham, at that time, was building pug walled houses and barns for people in the Gingin area. In 1857 Thomas Jnr got into altercations with a local Aboriginal man resulting in Thomas taking away the man's spears. According to Aboriginal law, this was punishable by a spearing in the leg which the Aboriginal man 'Gibena" did and Thomas was taken to hospital in Perth. Gibena was later tried for this offence and sentenced to 18 months prison with hard labour.[82] Just one of the doubtless many altercations with the Indigenous peoples where the latter came off worst.

Udell[83] states that in 1852 W.L. Brockman advertised a small farm on the eastern side of the Gingin Brook. This farm was called "Moraba" and the lease was taken up by Thomas & Mary where it is said that they established a very successful farm. In a somewhat contradictory statement, Udell then goes onto say that about 1854, Thomas Buckingham and Richard Cockram blazed a trail from Wanneroo to Gingin. Together they built pug-walled houses and barns for settlers along the Gingin Brook. In 1861

---

[81] Neergabby a history of the Moore River and Lower Gingin Brook" W.J. de Burgh 1976 Shire of Singin
[82] Perth Gazette Jan 8th 1858 p3
[83] Gingin 1830-1960" by Hazel Udell 1979 Shire of Gingin.

Thomas Buckingham is recorded as being a donor to the building fund for St Luke's Church, Gingin.[84]

By 1866 Thomas and Mary are known to have been in Kelmscott. A newspaper article entitled "Historic Kelmscott Another Centenary Celebration" page 4[85] talks about how Thomas along with his sons, was responsible for building the first water mill in the district. This was built on the Canning River at Roleystone in 1866 just as was recorded in Thomas Jnr's memoirs.

Mary died in 1875 aged 60 and two years later, in 1877 Thomas married Elizabeth Plackett[86]

Two years after this, Thomas died[87] at Roleystone and is buried at Saint Mary-in-the-Valley Church Cemetery[88]

---

[84] "Inquirer, 27th March 1861"
[85] The West Australian (Perth W.A. 1879-1954) Saturday 10th January 1931
[86] Australian Marriage Index, 1788-1950 Ancestry.com.au
[87] Australian Death Index, 1787-1985 Ancestry.com.au
[88] Australia and New Zealand, Find a Grave Index, 1800-current Ancestry.com.au

Children of Thomas Buckingham and Mary Chanter

Maria 1836-1919	m Edward Bentley
	m John Thomas
Thomas 1839-1913	m Hannah Salter
Mary 1841-1921	m Edmund Oxenham Cockram
Alexander 1843-1897	m Elizabeth York
Betsy 1847-1925	m Edwin Cockram
Caroline 1849-1915	m Charles Fancoat
William 1853-1917	m Sarah Jane Holt
Ellen 1856-1878	m Samuel Salter
John 1858-1947	m Emily amelia Okely
Hugh James 1860-1940	m Hudia Elizabeth Matthiesson

My lineage from Thomas Buckingham and Mary Chanter
Maria Buckingham who married John Thomas
Frederick Charles Thomas who married Frances Ann Isabel York
Alfred Donald (Don) Thomas who married Maud M Pratt

SUMMARY

In summary then, as I look back to the reasons that led me to write about these particular people, it was the fact that they all came out from England to Western Australia and they all ended up among the early settlers of Gingin.

I still think this is quite amazing. Give the small numbers of early settlers, they all would have known each other and many had properties bordering on each other or they rented houses off each other and certainly they married each other. For example, the two Edward brothers, Matthew (1825-1916) and Joshua (1820-1866) married sisters Annie (1835-1879) and Emma (1828-1901) King. William Adams York (1856-1933) married Amy Elizabeth Edwards (1854-1922). Alexander Buckingham (1843-1897) married Elizabeth York (1850-1940). Maria Buckingham (1836-1919) married John Thomas (1829-1920). Alice Thomas (1867-1934) married John Buckingham (186401926) and Flora Thomas (1860-1942 married Herbert Matthew Edwards (1860-1942). How confusing is this!

In 1881 a census for Gingin was conducted and the population was assessed as being 51 males and 46 females[89]. The Kings, Edwards, Yorks and John Thomas were all listed but of course

---

[89] Gingin 1830-1960 by Hazel Udell 1979 Shire of Gingin

the Buckinghams had moved to Roleystone by this time. Given their large families, it would seem that our ancestors made a good proportion of the entire population of Gingin.

Not only did these pioneers have to clear their land, build their homes, do all their fencing but they also found time to be engaged as responsible citizens. By 1860, all of them are listed as donors to the building fund for St Luke's Church, Gingin. Thomas Buckingham, Joshua and Matthew Edwards, John York, John Thomas, Richard King and Daniel King.[90] They also served on the Gingin Road Board which was formed in 1893. Here, at this later date, we are looking mainly at the children of our pioneer families.

Apparently, Gingin has always been renowned for its beef cattle. Ever since W.L. Brockman brought them to the area in the early 1840's.[1] Udell reports that Joshua Edwards, Samuel Mortimer and John York all ran herds during this period. John York at Creaton, was also known to have a herd of dairy cows. Udell quotes the Inquirer of 1880 which reported over 14,000 bushels of wheat was to be harvested in Gingin that year. Udell further reports (p145) that in 1882 John Dewer, who married Selena York, bought John York's property (145) which included the homesteads of Creaton and Breara plus the land called Spratton. He paid 4,500 pounds and this included the live-stock. John York Snr is reported to have retired and moved into Gingin town where he lived until his death in 1896. Still reading Udell, she reports that as early as "1880 a group of Gingin residents met at Reuben Edwards Gingin Hotel on Weld Street" p147 to discuss the idea of a railway from Perth which was completed in 1891. A number of farmers lost a lot of their grazing land for this railway. Richard King lost 6,200 acres and Daniel King lost 8,400 acres.

---

[90] The Inquirer, 27th March, 1861.

I hope you have enjoyed reading about your early ancestors in this area and I really hope that you take the time to visit this old historic township of Gingin. It is a lovely place.

Kay

www.ingramcontent.com/pod-product-compliance
Lightning Source LLC
LaVergne TN
LVHW011856060526
838200LV00054B/4365